Y0-CRG-718

Steve Jobs

Jennifer Strand

abdopublishing.com

Published by Abdo Zoom™, PO Box 398166, Minneapolis, Minnesota 55439. Copyright © 2017 by Abdo Consulting Group, Inc. International copyrights reserved in all countries. No part of this book may be reproduced in any form without written permission from the publisher. Abdo Zoom™ is a trademark and logo of Abdo Consulting Group, Inc.

Printed in the United States of America, North Mankato, Minnesota
092016
012017

THIS BOOK CONTAINS
RECYCLED MATERIALS

Cover Photo: Paul Sakuma/AP Images
Interior Photos: Paul Sakuma/AP Images, 1, 12, 16, 18; Jeff Chiu/AP Images, 4; Shutterstock Images, 5, 17; iStockphoto, 6–7; Seth Poppel/Yearbook Library, 7; Sal Veder/AP Images, 8–9; Eric Risberg/AP Images, 11; Lou Dematteis/Reuters/Newscom, 13; Siegle Jochen/Picture-Alliance/DPA/AP Images, 15; Richard Lewis/AP Images, 19

Editor: Brienna Rossiter
Series Designer: Madeline Berger
Art Direction: Dorothy Toth

Publisher's Cataloging-in-Publication Data
Names: Strand, Jennifer, author.
Title: Steve Jobs / by Jennifer Strand.
Description: Minneapolis, MN : Abdo Zoom, 2017. | Series: Technology pioneers | Includes bibliographical references and index.
Identifiers: LCCN 2016948914 | ISBN 9781680799279 (lib. bdg.) | ISBN 9781624025136 (ebook) | 9781624025693 (Read-to-me ebook)
Subjects: LCSH: Jobs, Steve, 1955-2011--Juvenile literature. | Computer engineers--United States--Biography--Juvenile literature. | Businessmen--United States--History--Juvenile literature. | Apple Computer, Inc.--History--Juvenile literature.
Classification: DDC 338.7/610054092 [B]--dc23
LC record available at http://lccn.loc.gov/2016948914

Table of Contents

Steve Jobs helped found Apple. Apple helped make personal computers **popular**.

It also made new personal devices
such as iPods and iPhones.

Steve was born on February 24, 1955.
He grew up in California.
He liked **electronics**.

He worked for
a video game company.

Jobs worked with his friend Steve Wozniak.

8

They made computer parts. They also started a computer business. It was called Apple Computer Inc.

They made a computer in 1977. It was called the Apple II. It was easy to use. This made it popular.

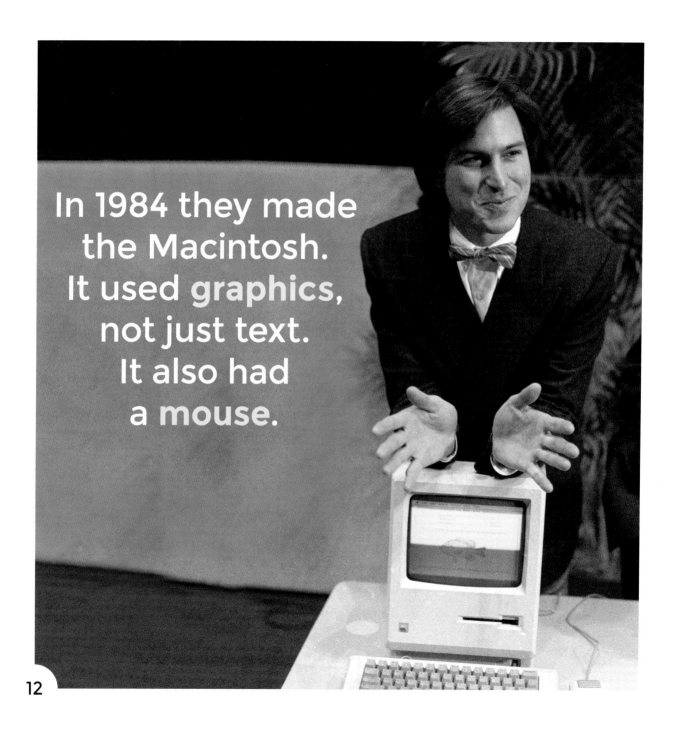

In 1984 they made
the Macintosh.
It used **graphics**,
not just text.
It also had
a **mouse**.

Later Apple made laptops, too.

History Maker

In 2001 Apple released the iPod.
It was a tiny music player.
It held hundreds of songs.
People could **download** songs
from Apple's iTunes store.

Apple became very successful. Many people bought music from iTunes.

Later Apple made the iPhone and the iPad. They had touchscreens.

Jobs died on October 5, 2011.

His company changed the way people use technology. It helped make computers and other devices part of everyday life.

Steve Jobs

Born: February 24, 1955

Birthplace: San Francisco, California

Wife: Laurene Powell

Known For: Jobs helped found Apple. Apple makes personal computers and devices.

Died: October 5, 2011

Key Dates

1955: Stephen Paul Jobs is born on February 24.

1976: Jobs and Steve Wozniak start Apple Computer Inc.

1977: The Apple II computer is released.

2001: Apple introduces the iPod.

2007: Apple releases the iPhone.

2011: Jobs dies on October 5.

Glossary

download - to move a file from the Internet to a computer or device.

electronics - devices (such as computers, TVs, and radios) with many small electrical parts.

graphics - images such as drawings or maps.

mouse - a small device that controls the pointer on a computer screen.

popular - liked or enjoyed by many people.

Booklinks

For more information
on **Steve Jobs**, please visit
booklinks.abdopublishing.com

Z⚲m **In on Biographies!**

Learn even more with the Abdo Zoom
Biographies database. Check out
abdozoom.com for more information.

Index